This planner belongs to :

_____

Twenty-four
20

January
S	M	T	W	T	F	S
	1	2	3	4	5	6
7	8	9	10	11	12	13
14	15	16	17	18	19	20
21	22	23	24	25	26	27
28	29	30	31			

February
S	M	T	W	T	F	S
				1	2	3
4	5	6	7	8	9	10
11	12	13	14	15	16	17
18	19	20	21	22	23	24
25	26	27	28	29		

March
S	M	T	W	T	F	S
					1	2
3	4	5	6	7	8	9
10	11	12	13	14	15	16
17	18	19	20	21	22	23
24	25	26	27	28	29	30
31						

April
S	M	T	W	T	F	S
	1	2	3	4	5	6
7	8	9	10	11	12	13
14	15	16	17	18	19	20
21	22	23	24	25	26	27
28	29	30				

May
S	M	T	W	T	F	S
			1	2	3	4
5	6	7	8	9	10	11
12	13	14	15	16	17	18
19	20	21	22	23	24	25
26	27	28	29	30	31	

June
S	M	T	W	T	F	S
						1
2	3	4	5	6	7	8
9	10	11	12	13	14	15
16	17	18	19	20	21	22
23	24	25	26	27	28	29
30						

July
S	M	T	W	T	F	S
	1	2	3	4	5	6
7	8	9	10	11	12	13
14	15	16	17	18	19	20
21	22	23	24	25	26	27
28	29	30	31			

August
S	M	T	W	T	F	S
				1	2	3
4	5	6	7	8	9	10
11	12	13	14	15	16	17
18	19	20	21	22	23	24
25	26	27	28	29	30	31

September
S	M	T	W	T	F	S
1	2	3	4	5	6	7
8	9	10	11	12	13	14
15	16	17	18	19	20	21
22	23	24	25	26	27	28
29	30					

October
S	M	T	W	T	F	S
		1	2	3	4	5
6	7	8	9	10	11	12
13	14	15	16	17	18	19
20	21	22	23	24	25	26
27	28	29	30	31		

November
S	M	T	W	T	F	S
					1	2
3	4	5	6	7	8	9
10	11	12	13	14	15	16
17	18	19	20	21	22	23
24	25	26	27	28	29	30

December
S	M	T	W	T	F	S
1	2	3	4	5	6	7
8	9	10	11	12	13	14
15	16	17	18	19	20	21
22	23	24	25	26	27	28
29	30	31				

Year in Pixels

	J	F	M	A	M	J	J	A	S	O	N	D
1.												
2.												
3.												
4.												
5.												
6.												
7.												
8.												
9.												
10.												
11.												
12.												
13.												
14.												
15.												
16.												
17.												
18.												
19.												
20.												
21.												
22.												
23.												
24.												
25.												
26.												
27.												
28.												
29.												
30.												
31.												

Color Codes

Notes

January

MONDAY	TUESDAY	WEDNESDAY	THURSDAY
1	2	3	4
8	9	10	11
15	16	17	18
22	23	24	25
29	30	31	

January 2024

FRIDAY	SATURDAY	SUNDAY	NOTES
5	6	7	○
			○
			○
			○
			○
12	13	14	○
			○
			○
			○
19	20	21	○
			○
			○
			○
			○
26	27	28	○
			○
			○
			○
			○
			NOTES

February 2024

MONDAY	TUESDAY	WEDNESDAY	THURSDAY
			1
5	6	7	8
12	13	14	15
19	20	21	22
26	27	28	29

February

2024

FRIDAY	SATURDAY	SUNDAY	NOTES
2	3	4	○
			○
			○
			○
9	10	11	○
			○
			○
			○
			○
16	17	18	○
			○
			○
			○
			○
23	24	25	○
			○
			○
			○
			○
			NOTES

March 2024

MONDAY	TUESDAY	WEDNESDAY	THURSDAY
4	5	6	7
11	12	13	14
18	19	20	21
25	26	27	28

March

2024

FRIDAY	SATURDAY	SUNDAY	NOTES
1	2	3	○
			○
			○
			○
			○
8	9	10	○
			○
			○
			○
15	16	17	○
			○
			○
			○
			○
22	23	24	○
			○
			○
			○
			○
29	30	31	NOTES

April 2024

MONDAY	TUESDAY	WEDNESDAY	THURSDAY
1	2	3	4
8	9	10	11
15	16	17	18
22	23	24	25
29	30		

April

2024

FRIDAY	SATURDAY	SUNDAY	NOTES
5	6	7	○
			○
			○
			○
			○
12	13	14	○
			○
			○
			○
19	20	21	○
			○
			○
			○
			○
26	27	28	○
			○
			○
			○
			○
			NOTES

May

MONDAY	TUESDAY	WEDNESDAY	THURSDAY
		1	2
6	7	8	9
13	14	15	16
20	21	22	23
27	28	29	30

May

2024

FRIDAY	SATURDAY	SUNDAY	NOTES
3	4	5	○
			○
			○
			○
			○
10	11	12	○
			○
			○
			○
17	18	19	○
			○
			○
			○
			○
24	25	26	○
			○
			○
			○
			○
31			NOTES

June

MONDAY	TUESDAY	WEDNESDAY	THURSDAY
3	4	5	6
10	11	12	13
17	18	19	20
24	25	26	27

June

FRIDAY	SATURDAY	SUNDAY	NOTES
	1	2	○
			○
			○
			○
			○
7	8	9	○
			○
			○
			○
14	15	16	○
			○
			○
			○
			○
21	22	23	○
			○
			○
			○
			○
28	29	30	NOTES

July

MONDAY	TUESDAY	WEDNESDAY	THURSDAY
1	2	3	4
8	9	10	11
15	16	17	18
22	23	24	25
29	30	31	

July 2024

FRIDAY	SATURDAY	SUNDAY	NOTES
5	6	7	○
			○
			○
			○
			○
12	13	14	○
			○
			○
			○
19	20	21	○
			○
			○
			○
			○
26	27	28	○
			○
			○
			○
			○
			NOTES

August

2024

MONDAY	TUESDAY	WEDNESDAY	THURSDAY
			1
5	6	7	8
12	13	14	15
19	20	21	22
26	27	28	29

August

2024

FRIDAY	SATURDAY	SUNDAY	NOTES
2	3	4	○
			○
			○
			○
9	10	11	○
			○
			○
			○
			○
16	17	18	○
			○
			○
			○
			○
23	24	25	○
			○
			○
			○
			○
30	31		NOTES

September

MONDAY	TUESDAY	WEDNESDAY	THURSDAY
2	3	4	5
9	10	11	12
16	17	18	19
23	24	25	26

September

2024

FRIDAY	SATURDAY	SUNDAY	NOTES
		1	○
			○
			○
			○
			○
6	7	8	○
			○
			○
			○
13	14	15	○
			○
			○
			○
			○
20	21	22	○
			○
			○
			○
			○
27	28	29	30

October

2024

MONDAY	TUESDAY	WEDNESDAY	THURSDAY
	1	2	3
7	8	9	10
14	15	16	17
21	22	23	24
28	29	30	31

October

FRIDAY	SATURDAY	SUNDAY	NOTES
4	5	6	○
			○
			○
			○
			○
11	12	13	○
			○
			○
			○
18	19	20	○
			○
			○
			○
			○
25	26	27	○
			○
			○
			○
			○
			NOTES

November 2024

MONDAY	TUESDAY	WEDNESDAY	THURSDAY
4	5	6	7
11	12	13	14
18	19	20	21
25	26	27	28

November
2024

FRIDAY	SATURDAY	SUNDAY	NOTES
1	2	3	○
			○
			○
			○
			○
8	9	10	○
			○
			○
			○
15	16	17	○
			○
			○
			○
			○
22	23	24	○
			○
			○
			○
			○
29	30		NOTES

December 2024

MONDAY	TUESDAY	WEDNESDAY	THURSDAY
2	3	4	5
9	10	11	12
16	17	18	19
23	24	25	26

December 2024

FRIDAY	SATURDAY	SUNDAY	NOTES
		1	○
			○
			○
			○
6	7	8	○
			○
			○
			○
			○
13	14	15	○
			○
			○
			○
			○
20	21	22	○
			○
			○
			○
			○
27	28	29	30 / 31

December
2023

01 FRIDAY
- ○ _____
- ○ _____
- ○ _____
- ○ _____
- ○ _____
- ○ _____
- ○ _____
- ○ _____

02 SATURDAY
- ○ _____
- ○ _____
- ○ _____
- ○ _____
- ○ _____
- ○ _____
- ○ _____
- ○ _____

03 SUNDAY
- ○ _____
- ○ _____
- ○ _____
- ○ _____
- ○ _____
- ○ _____
- ○ _____
- ○ _____

04 MONDAY
- ○ _____
- ○ _____
- ○ _____
- ○ _____
- ○ _____

05 TUESDAY

○ _____
○ _____
○ _____
○ _____
○ _____
○ _____
○ _____
○ _____

06 WEDNESDAY

○ _____
○ _____
○ _____
○ _____
○ _____
○ _____
○ _____
○ _____

07 THURSDAY

○ _____
○ _____
○ _____
○ _____
○ _____
○ _____
○ _____
○ _____

08 FRIDAY

○ _____
○ _____
○ _____
○ _____
○ _____

09 SATURDAY

○ _____
○ _____
○ _____
○ _____
○ _____
○ _____
○ _____
○ _____

10 SUNDAY

○ _____
○ _____
○ _____
○ _____
○ _____
○ _____
○ _____
○ _____

11 MONDAY

○ _____
○ _____
○ _____
○ _____
○ _____
○ _____
○ _____
○ _____

12 TUESDAY

○ _____
○ _____
○ _____
○ _____
○ _____

13 WEDNESDAY

14 THURSDAY

15 FRIDAY

16 SATURDAY

17 SUNDAY

18 MONDAY

19 TUESDAY

20 WEDNESDAY

December
2023

21 THURSDAY

○
○
○
○
○
○
○
○

22 FRIDAY

○
○
○
○
○
○
○
○

23 SATURDAY

○
○
○
○
○
○
○
○

24 SUNDAY

○
○
○
○
○

25 MONDAY

○ _____
○ _____
○ _____
○ _____
○ _____
○ _____
○ _____
○ _____

26 TUESDAY

○ _____
○ _____
○ _____
○ _____
○ _____
○ _____
○ _____
○ _____

27 WEDNESDAY

○ _____
○ _____
○ _____
○ _____
○ _____
○ _____
○ _____
○ _____

28 THURSDAY

○ _____
○ _____
○ _____
○ _____
○ _____

29 FRIDAY

○ _____
○ _____
○ _____
○ _____
○ _____
○ _____
○ _____
○ _____

30 SATURDAY

○ _____
○ _____
○ _____
○ _____
○ _____
○ _____
○ _____
○ _____

31 SUNDAY

○ _____
○ _____
○ _____
○ _____
○ _____
○ _____
○ _____
○ _____

NOTES

_____
_____
_____
_____

January 2024

01 MONDAY

- ○ _____
- ○ _____
- ○ _____
- ○ _____
- ○ _____
- ○ _____
- ○ _____
- ○ _____

02 TUESDAY

- ○ _____
- ○ _____
- ○ _____
- ○ _____
- ○ _____
- ○ _____
- ○ _____
- ○ _____

03 WEDNESDAY

- ○ _____
- ○ _____
- ○ _____
- ○ _____
- ○ _____
- ○ _____
- ○ _____
- ○ _____

04 THURSDAY

- ○ _____
- ○ _____
- ○ _____
- ○ _____
- ○ _____

05 FRIDAY

○ _____
○ _____
○ _____
○ _____
○ _____
○ _____
○ _____
○ _____

06 SATURDAY

○ _____
○ _____
○ _____
○ _____
○ _____
○ _____
○ _____
○ _____

07 SUNDAY

○ _____
○ _____
○ _____
○ _____
○ _____
○ _____
○ _____
○ _____

08 MONDAY

○ _____
○ _____
○ _____
○ _____
○ _____

09 TUESDAY

○ _____
○ _____
○ _____
○ _____
○ _____
○ _____
○ _____
○ _____

10 WEDNESDAY

○ _____
○ _____
○ _____
○ _____
○ _____
○ _____
○ _____
○ _____

11 THURSDAY

○ _____
○ _____
○ _____
○ _____
○ _____
○ _____
○ _____
○ _____

12 FRIDAY

○ _____
○ _____
○ _____
○ _____
○ _____

13 SATURDAY

○ _____
○ _____
○ _____
○ _____
○ _____
○ _____
○ _____
○ _____

14 SUNDAY

○ _____
○ _____
○ _____
○ _____
○ _____
○ _____
○ _____
○ _____

15 MONDAY

○ _____
○ _____
○ _____
○ _____
○ _____
○ _____
○ _____
○ _____

16 TUESDAY

○ _____
○ _____
○ _____
○ _____
○ _____

17 WEDNESDAY

○ _____
○ _____
○ _____
○ _____
○ _____
○ _____
○ _____
○ _____

18 THURSDAY

○ _____
○ _____
○ _____
○ _____
○ _____
○ _____
○ _____
○ _____

19 FRIDAY

○ _____
○ _____
○ _____
○ _____
○ _____
○ _____
○ _____
○ _____

20 SATURDAY

○ _____
○ _____
○ _____
○ _____
○ _____

21 SUNDAY
○ _____
○ _____
○ _____
○ _____
○ _____
○ _____
○ _____
○ _____

22 MONDAY
○ _____
○ _____
○ _____
○ _____
○ _____
○ _____
○ _____
○ _____

23 TUESDAY
○ _____
○ _____
○ _____
○ _____
○ _____
○ _____
○ _____
○ _____

24 WEDNESDAY
○ _____
○ _____
○ _____
○ _____
○ _____

25 THURSDAY

○ _____
○ _____
○ _____
○ _____
○ _____
○ _____
○ _____
○ _____

26 FRIDAY

○ _____
○ _____
○ _____
○ _____
○ _____
○ _____
○ _____
○ _____

27 SATURDAY

○ _____
○ _____
○ _____
○ _____
○ _____
○ _____
○ _____
○ _____

28 SUNDAY

○ _____
○ _____
○ _____
○ _____
○ _____

January 2024

29 MONDAY

○ _____
○ _____
○ _____
○ _____
○ _____
○ _____
○ _____
○ _____

30 TUESDAY

○ _____
○ _____
○ _____
○ _____
○ _____
○ _____
○ _____
○ _____

31 WEDNESDAY

○ _____
○ _____
○ _____
○ _____
○ _____
○ _____
○ _____
○ _____

NOTES

_____
_____
_____
_____
_____

February
2024

01 THURSDAY
- ○
- ○
- ○
- ○
- ○
- ○
- ○
- ○

02 FRIDAY
- ○
- ○
- ○
- ○
- ○
- ○
- ○
- ○

03 SATURDAY
- ○
- ○
- ○
- ○
- ○
- ○
- ○
- ○

04 SUNDAY
- ○
- ○
- ○
- ○
- ○

February 2024

05 MONDAY
- ○ _____
- ○ _____
- ○ _____
- ○ _____
- ○ _____
- ○ _____
- ○ _____
- ○ _____

06 TUESDAY
- ○ _____
- ○ _____
- ○ _____
- ○ _____
- ○ _____
- ○ _____
- ○ _____
- ○ _____

07 WEDNESDAY
- ○ _____
- ○ _____
- ○ _____
- ○ _____
- ○ _____
- ○ _____
- ○ _____
- ○ _____

08 THURSDAY
- ○ _____
- ○ _____
- ○ _____
- ○ _____
- ○ _____

February
2024

09 FRIDAY

○ _____
○ _____
○ _____
○ _____
○ _____
○ _____
○ _____
○ _____

10 SATURDAY

○ _____
○ _____
○ _____
○ _____
○ _____
○ _____
○ _____
○ _____

11 SUNDAY

○ _____
○ _____
○ _____
○ _____
○ _____
○ _____
○ _____
○ _____

12 MONDAY

○ _____
○ _____
○ _____
○ _____
○ _____

13 TUESDAY

○
○ _____
○
○ _____
○
○ _____
○
○ _____

14 WEDNESDAY

○
○ _____
○
○ _____
○
○ _____
○
○ _____
○
○ _____

15 THURSDAY

○
○ _____
○
○ _____
○
○ _____
○
○ _____

16 FRIDAY

○
○ _____
○
○ _____
○

17 SATURDAY

○ _____
○ _____
○ _____
○ _____
○ _____
○ _____
○ _____
○ _____

18 SUNDAY

○ _____
○ _____
○ _____
○ _____
○ _____
○ _____
○ _____
○ _____

19 MONDAY

○ _____
○ _____
○ _____
○ _____
○ _____
○ _____
○ _____
○ _____

20 TUESDAY

○ _____
○ _____
○ _____
○ _____
○ _____

21 WEDNESDAY
○ _____
○ _____
○ _____
○ _____
○ _____
○ _____
○ _____
○ _____

22 THURSDAY
○ _____
○ _____
○ _____
○ _____
○ _____
○ _____
○ _____
○ _____

23 FRIDAY
○ _____
○ _____
○ _____
○ _____
○ _____
○ _____
○ _____
○ _____

24 SATURDAY
○ _____
○ _____
○ _____
○ _____
○ _____

25 SUNDAY

○ _____
○ _____
○ _____
○ _____
○ _____
○ _____
○ _____
○ _____

26 MONDAY

○ _____
○ _____
○ _____
○ _____
○ _____
○ _____
○ _____
○ _____

27 TUESDAY

○ _____
○ _____
○ _____
○ _____
○ _____
○ _____
○ _____
○ _____

28 WEDNESDAY

○ _____
○ _____
○ _____
○ _____
○ _____

29 THURSDAY

○ _____
○ _____
○ _____
○ _____
○ _____
○ _____
○ _____
○ _____

NOTES

_____
_____
_____
_____
_____
_____
_____
_____
_____
_____
_____
_____
_____
_____
_____
_____
_____

March
2024

01 FRIDAY

○ _____
○ _____
○ _____
○ _____
○ _____
○ _____
○ _____
○ _____

02 SATURDAY

○ _____
○ _____
○ _____
○ _____
○ _____
○ _____
○ _____
○ _____

03 SUNDAY

○ _____
○ _____
○ _____
○ _____
○ _____
○ _____
○ _____
○ _____

04 MONDAY

○ _____
○ _____
○ _____
○ _____
○ _____

05 TUESDAY

○
○
○
○
○
○
○
○

06 WEDNESDAY

○
○
○
○
○
○
○
○

07 THURSDAY

○
○
○
○
○
○
○
○

08 FRIDAY

○
○
○
○
○

09 SATURDAY

○
○
○
○
○
○
○
○

10 SUNDAY

○
○
○
○
○
○
○
○

11 MONDAY

○
○
○
○
○
○
○
○

12 TUESDAY

○
○
○
○
○

13 WEDNESDAY

○
○
○
○
○
○
○
○

14 THURSDAY

○
○
○
○
○
○
○
○
○

15 FRIDAY

○
○
○
○
○
○
○
○

16 SATURDAY

○
○
○
○
○

March
2024

17 SUNDAY

18 MONDAY

19 TUESDAY

20 WEDNESDAY

21 THURSDAY

○ _____
○ _____
○ _____
○ _____
○ _____
○ _____
○ _____
○ _____

22 FRIDAY

○ _____
○ _____
○ _____
○ _____
○ _____
○ _____
○ _____
○ _____

23 SATURDAY

○ _____
○ _____
○ _____
○ _____
○ _____
○ _____
○ _____
○ _____

24 SUNDAY

○ _____
○ _____
○ _____
○ _____
○ _____

25 MONDAY

○ _____
○ _____
○ _____
○ _____
○ _____
○ _____
○ _____
○ _____

26 TUESDAY

○ _____
○ _____
○ _____
○ _____
○ _____
○ _____
○ _____
○ _____

27 WEDNESDAY

○ _____
○ _____
○ _____
○ _____
○ _____
○ _____
○ _____
○ _____

28 THURSDAY

○ _____
○ _____
○ _____
○ _____
○ _____

29 FRIDAY

○ _____
○ _____
○ _____
○ _____
○ _____
○ _____
○ _____
○ _____

30 SATURDAY

○ _____
○ _____
○ _____
○ _____
○ _____
○ _____
○ _____
○ _____

31 SUNDAY

○ _____
○ _____
○ _____
○ _____
○ _____
○ _____
○ _____
○ _____

NOTES

_____
_____
_____
_____

April
2024

01 MONDAY
- ○
- ○
- ○
- ○
- ○
- ○
- ○
- ○

02 TUESDAY
- ○
- ○
- ○
- ○
- ○
- ○
- ○
- ○

03 WEDNESDAY
- ○
- ○
- ○
- ○
- ○
- ○
- ○
- ○

04 THURSDAY
- ○
- ○
- ○
- ○
- ○

April
2024

05 FRIDAY
- ○
- ○
- ○
- ○
- ○
- ○
- ○
- ○

06 SATURDAY
- ○
- ○
- ○
- ○
- ○
- ○
- ○
- ○

07 SUNDAY
- ○
- ○
- ○
- ○
- ○
- ○
- ○
- ○

08 MONDAY
- ○
- ○
- ○
- ○
- ○

09 TUESDAY

○ _____
○ _____
○ _____
○ _____
○ _____
○ _____
○ _____
○ _____

10 WEDNESDAY

○ _____
○ _____
○ _____
○ _____
○ _____
○ _____
○ _____
○ _____

11 THURSDAY

○ _____
○ _____
○ _____
○ _____
○ _____
○ _____
○ _____
○ _____

12 FRIDAY

○ _____
○ _____
○ _____
○ _____
○ _____

13 SATURDAY

○ _____
○ _____
○ _____
○ _____
○ _____
○ _____
○ _____
○ _____

14 SUNDAY

○ _____
○ _____
○ _____
○ _____
○ _____
○ _____
○ _____
○ _____

15 MONDAY

○ _____
○ _____
○ _____
○ _____
○ _____
○ _____
○ _____
○ _____

16 TUESDAY

○ _____
○ _____
○ _____
○ _____
○ _____

17 WEDNESDAY

○ _____
○ _____
○ _____
○ _____
○ _____
○ _____
○ _____
○ _____

18 THURSDAY

○ _____
○ _____
○ _____
○ _____
○ _____
○ _____
○ _____
○ _____

19 FRIDAY

○ _____
○ _____
○ _____
○ _____
○ _____
○ _____
○ _____
○ _____

20 SATURDAY

○ _____
○ _____
○ _____
○ _____
○ _____

21 SUNDAY

○ _____
○ _____
○ _____
○ _____
○ _____
○ _____
○ _____
○ _____

22 MONDAY

○ _____
○ _____
○ _____
○ _____
○ _____
○ _____
○ _____
○ _____

23 TUESDAY

○ _____
○ _____
○ _____
○ _____
○ _____
○ _____
○ _____
○ _____

24 WEDNESDAY

○ _____
○ _____
○ _____
○ _____
○ _____

25 THURSDAY

○ _____
○ _____
○ _____
○ _____
○ _____
○ _____
○ _____
○ _____

26 FRIDAY

○ _____
○ _____
○ _____
○ _____
○ _____
○ _____
○ _____
○ _____

27 SATURDAY

○ _____
○ _____
○ _____
○ _____
○ _____
○ _____
○ _____
○ _____

28 SUNDAY

○ _____
○ _____
○ _____
○ _____
○ _____

April
2024

29 MONDAY
○
○
○
○
○
○
○
○

30 TUESDAY
○
○
○
○
○
○
○
○

NOTES

01 WEDNESDAY

○
○
○
○
○
○
○
○

02 THURSDAY

○
○
○
○
○
○
○
○

03 FRIDAY

○
○
○
○
○
○
○
○

04 SATURDAY

○
○
○
○
○

May
2024

05 SUNDAY
- ○
- ○
- ○
- ○
- ○
- ○
- ○
- ○

06 MONDAY
- ○
- ○
- ○
- ○
- ○
- ○
- ○
- ○

07 TUESDAY
- ○
- ○
- ○
- ○
- ○
- ○
- ○
- ○

08 WEDNESDAY
- ○
- ○
- ○
- ○
- ○

May
2024

09 THURSDAY
○ _____
○ _____
○ _____
○ _____
○ _____
○ _____
○ _____
○ _____

10 FRIDAY
○ _____
○ _____
○ _____
○ _____
○ _____
○ _____
○ _____
○ _____

11 SATURDAY
○ _____
○ _____
○ _____
○ _____
○ _____
○ _____
○ _____
○ _____

12 SUNDAY
○ _____
○ _____
○ _____
○ _____
○ _____

13 MONDAY

○
○
○
○
○
○
○
○

14 TUESDAY

○
○
○
○
○
○
○
○
○

15 WEDNESDAY

○
○
○
○
○
○
○
○

16 THURSDAY

○
○
○
○
○

17 FRIDAY

○ _____
○ _____
○ _____
○ _____
○ _____
○ _____
○ _____
○ _____

18 SATURDAY

○ _____
○ _____
○ _____
○ _____
○ _____
○ _____
○ _____
○ _____

19 SUNDAY

○ _____
○ _____
○ _____
○ _____
○ _____
○ _____
○ _____
○ _____

20 MONDAY

○ _____
○ _____
○ _____
○ _____
○ _____

21 TUESDAY

○
○
○
○
○
○
○
○

22 WEDNESDAY

○
○
○
○
○
○
○
○

23 THURSDAY

○
○
○
○
○
○
○
○

24 FRIDAY

○
○
○
○
○

25 SATURDAY

○
○
○
○
○
○
○
○

26 SUNDAY

○
○
○
○
○
○
○
○

27 MONDAY

○
○
○
○
○
○
○
○

28 TUESDAY

○
○
○
○
○

May
2024

29 WEDNESDAY

○ _____
○ _____
○ _____
○ _____
○ _____
○ _____
○ _____
○ _____

30 THURSDAY

○ _____
○ _____
○ _____
○ _____
○ _____
○ _____
○ _____
○ _____

31 FRIDAY

○ _____
○ _____
○ _____
○ _____
○ _____
○ _____
○ _____
○ _____

NOTES

_____
_____
_____
_____

June 2024

01 SATURDAY
- ○ _____
- ○ _____
- ○ _____
- ○ _____
- ○ _____
- ○ _____
- ○ _____
- ○ _____

02 SUNDAY
- ○ _____
- ○ _____
- ○ _____
- ○ _____
- ○ _____
- ○ _____
- ○ _____
- ○ _____

03 MONDAY
- ○ _____
- ○ _____
- ○ _____
- ○ _____
- ○ _____
- ○ _____
- ○ _____
- ○ _____

04 TUESDAY
- ○ _____
- ○ _____
- ○ _____
- ○ _____
- ○ _____

05 WEDNESDAY

○
○
○
○
○
○
○
○

06 THURSDAY

○
○
○
○
○
○
○
○

07 FRIDAY

○
○
○
○
○
○
○
○

08 SATURDAY

○
○
○
○
○

09 SUNDAY
○ _____
○ _____
○ _____
○ _____
○ _____
○ _____
○ _____
○ _____

10 MONDAY
○ _____
○ _____
○ _____
○ _____
○ _____
○ _____
○ _____
○ _____

11 TUESDAY
○ _____
○ _____
○ _____
○ _____
○ _____
○ _____
○ _____
○ _____

12 WEDNESDAY
○ _____
○ _____
○ _____
○ _____
○ _____

13 THURSDAY

○
○ _____
○ _____
○ _____
○ _____
○ _____
○ _____
○ _____

14 FRIDAY

○
○ _____
○ _____
○ _____
○ _____
○ _____
○ _____
○ _____

15 SATURDAY

○
○ _____
○ _____
○ _____
○ _____
○ _____
○ _____
○ _____

16 SUNDAY

○
○ _____
○ _____
○ _____
○ _____

17 MONDAY

○
○
○
○
○
○
○
○

18 TUESDAY

○
○
○
○
○
○
○
○

19 WEDNESDAY

○
○
○
○
○
○
○
○

20 THURSDAY

○
○
○
○
○

21 FRIDAY

○
○
○
○
○
○
○
○

22 SATURDAY

○
○
○
○
○
○
○
○

23 SUNDAY

○
○
○
○
○
○
○
○

24 MONDAY

○
○
○
○
○

25 TUESDAY

○ _____
○ _____
○ _____
○ _____
○ _____
○ _____
○ _____
○ _____

26 WEDNESDAY

○ _____
○ _____
○ _____
○ _____
○ _____
○ _____
○ _____
○ _____

27 THURSDAY

○ _____
○ _____
○ _____
○ _____
○ _____
○ _____
○ _____
○ _____

28 FRIDAY

○ _____
○ _____
○ _____
○ _____
○ _____

29 SATURDAY

30 SUNDAY

NOTES

01 MONDAY

○ _____
○ _____
○ _____
○ _____
○ _____
○ _____
○ _____
○ _____

02 TUESDAY

○ _____
○ _____
○ _____
○ _____
○ _____
○ _____
○ _____
○ _____

03 WEDNESDAY

○ _____
○ _____
○ _____
○ _____
○ _____
○ _____
○ _____
○ _____

04 THURSDAY

○ _____
○ _____
○ _____
○ _____
○ _____

July 2024

05 FRIDAY
- ○
- ○
- ○
- ○
- ○
- ○
- ○
- ○

06 SATURDAY
- ○
- ○
- ○
- ○
- ○
- ○
- ○
- ○

07 SUNDAY
- ○
- ○
- ○
- ○
- ○
- ○
- ○
- ○

08 MONDAY
- ○
- ○
- ○
- ○
- ○

09 TUESDAY

○ _____
○ _____
○ _____
○ _____
○ _____
○ _____
○ _____
○ _____

10 WEDNESDAY

○ _____
○ _____
○ _____
○ _____
○ _____
○ _____
○ _____
○ _____

11 THURSDAY

○ _____
○ _____
○ _____
○ _____
○ _____
○ _____
○ _____
○ _____

12 FRIDAY

○ _____
○ _____
○ _____
○ _____
○ _____

13 SATURDAY

○
○
○
○
○
○
○
○

14 SUNDAY

○
○
○
○
○
○
○
○

15 MONDAY

○
○
○
○
○
○
○
○

16 TUESDAY

○
○
○
○
○

17 WEDNESDAY
○
○
○
○
○
○
○
○

18 THURSDAY
○
○
○
○
○
○
○
○

19 FRIDAY
○
○
○
○
○
○
○
○

20 SATURDAY
○
○
○
○
○

21 SUNDAY

○
○ _____
○ _____
○ _____
○ _____
○ _____
○ _____
○ _____

22 MONDAY

○
○ _____
○ _____
○ _____
○ _____
○ _____
○ _____
○ _____

23 TUESDAY

○
○ _____
○ _____
○ _____
○ _____
○ _____
○ _____
○ _____

24 WEDNESDAY

○
○ _____
○ _____
○ _____
○ _____

25 THURSDAY

○ _____
○ _____
○ _____
○ _____
○ _____
○ _____
○ _____
○ _____

26 FRIDAY

○ _____
○ _____
○ _____
○ _____
○ _____
○ _____
○ _____
○ _____

27 SATURDAY

○ _____
○ _____
○ _____
○ _____
○ _____
○ _____
○ _____
○ _____

28 SUNDAY

○ _____
○ _____
○ _____
○ _____
○ _____

July
2024

29 MONDAY
○
○
○
○
○
○
○
○

30 TUESDAY
○
○
○
○
○
○
○
○

31 WEDNESDAY
○
○
○
○
○
○
○
○

NOTES

01 THURSDAY

○ _____
○ _____
○ _____
○ _____
○ _____
○ _____
○ _____
○ _____

02 FRIDAY

○ _____
○ _____
○ _____
○ _____
○ _____
○ _____
○ _____
○ _____

03 SATURDAY

○ _____
○ _____
○ _____
○ _____
○ _____
○ _____
○ _____
○ _____

04 SUNDAY

○ _____
○ _____
○ _____
○ _____
○ _____

05 MONDAY

○
○
○
○
○
○
○
○

06 TUESDAY

○
○
○
○
○
○
○
○

07 WEDNESDAY

○
○
○
○
○
○
○
○

08 THURSDAY

○
○
○
○
○

09 FRIDAY

○
○
○
○
○
○
○
○

10 SATURDAY

○
○
○
○
○
○
○
○

11 SUNDAY

○
○
○
○
○
○
○
○

12 MONDAY

○
○
○
○
○

13 TUESDAY

○
○
○
○
○
○
○
○

14 WEDNESDAY

○
○
○
○
○
○
○
○

15 THURSDAY

○
○
○
○
○
○
○
○

16 FRIDAY

○
○
○
○
○

17 SATURDAY

○ _____
○ _____
○ _____
○ _____
○ _____
○ _____
○ _____
○ _____

18 SUNDAY

○ _____
○ _____
○ _____
○ _____
○ _____
○ _____
○ _____
○ _____

19 MONDAY

○ _____
○ _____
○ _____
○ _____
○ _____
○ _____
○ _____
○ _____

20 TUESDAY

○ _____
○ _____
○ _____
○ _____
○ _____

21 WEDNESDAY

○
○
○
○
○
○
○
○

22 THURSDAY

○
○
○
○
○
○
○
○

23 FRIDAY

○
○
○
○
○
○
○
○

24 SATURDAY

○
○
○
○
○

25 SUNDAY

26 MONDAY

27 TUESDAY

28 WEDNESDAY

August
2024

29 THURSDAY
○ _____
○ _____
○ _____
○ _____
○ _____
○ _____
○ _____
○ _____

30 FRIDAY
○ _____
○ _____
○ _____
○ _____
○ _____
○ _____
○ _____
○ _____
○ _____

31 SATURDAY
○ _____
○ _____
○ _____
○ _____
○ _____
○ _____
○ _____
○ _____

NOTES
_____
_____
_____
_____

September
2024

01 SUNDAY

○ _____
○ _____
○ _____
○ _____
○ _____
○ _____
○ _____
○ _____

02 MONDAY

○ _____
○ _____
○ _____
○ _____
○ _____
○ _____
○ _____
○ _____

03 TUESDAY

○ _____
○ _____
○ _____
○ _____
○ _____
○ _____
○ _____
○ _____

04 WEDNESDAY

○ _____
○ _____
○ _____
○ _____
○ _____

September
2024

05 THURSDAY

○
○
○
○
○
○
○
○

06 FRIDAY

○
○
○
○
○
○
○
○

07 SATURDAY

○
○
○
○
○
○
○
○

08 SUNDAY

○
○
○
○
○

09 MONDAY

○ _____
○ _____
○ _____
○ _____
○ _____
○ _____
○ _____
○ _____

10 TUESDAY

○ _____
○ _____
○ _____
○ _____
○ _____
○ _____
○ _____
○ _____

11 WEDNESDAY

○ _____
○ _____
○ _____
○ _____
○ _____
○ _____
○ _____
○ _____

12 THURSDAY

○ _____
○ _____
○ _____
○ _____
○ _____

13 FRIDAY
○
○
○
○
○
○
○
○

14 SATURDAY
○
○
○
○
○
○
○
○

15 SUNDAY
○
○
○
○
○
○
○
○

16 MONDAY
○
○
○
○
○

September
2024

17 TUESDAY
○
○
○
○
○
○
○
○

18 WEDNESDAY
○
○
○
○
○
○
○
○

19 THURSDAY
○
○
○
○
○
○
○
○

20 FRIDAY
○
○
○
○
○

21 SATURDAY

○ ─────────────────────────────────────
○ ─────────────────────────────────────
○ ─────────────────────────────────────
○ ─────────────────────────────────────
○ ─────────────────────────────────────
○ ─────────────────────────────────────
○ ─────────────────────────────────────
○ ─────────────────────────────────────

22 SUNDAY

○ ─────────────────────────────────────
○ ─────────────────────────────────────
○ ─────────────────────────────────────
○ ─────────────────────────────────────
○ ─────────────────────────────────────
○ ─────────────────────────────────────
○ ─────────────────────────────────────
○ ─────────────────────────────────────

23 MONDAY

○ ─────────────────────────────────────
○ ─────────────────────────────────────
○ ─────────────────────────────────────
○ ─────────────────────────────────────
○ ─────────────────────────────────────
○ ─────────────────────────────────────
○ ─────────────────────────────────────
○ ─────────────────────────────────────

24 TUESDAY

○ ─────────────────────────────────────
○ ─────────────────────────────────────
○ ─────────────────────────────────────
○ ─────────────────────────────────────
○ ─────────────────────────────────────

September
2024

25 WEDNESDAY

○
○
○
○
○
○
○
○

26 THURSDAY

○
○
○
○
○
○
○
○

27 FRIDAY

○
○
○
○
○
○
○
○

28 SATURDAY

○
○
○
○
○

September
2024

29 SUNDAY

○ _____
○ _____
○ _____
○ _____
○ _____
○ _____
○ _____
○ _____

30 MONDAY

○ _____
○ _____
○ _____
○ _____
○ _____
○ _____
○ _____
○ _____

NOTES

01 TUESDAY
○ _____
○ _____
○ _____
○ _____
○ _____
○ _____
○ _____
○ _____

02 WEDNESDAY
○ _____
○ _____
○ _____
○ _____
○ _____
○ _____
○ _____
○ _____

03 THURSDAY
○ _____
○ _____
○ _____
○ _____
○ _____
○ _____
○ _____
○ _____

04 FRIDAY
○ _____
○ _____
○ _____
○ _____
○ _____

05 SATURDAY
○
○
○
○
○
○
○
○

06 SUNDAY
○
○
○
○
○
○
○
○

07 MONDAY
○
○
○
○
○
○
○
○

08 TUESDAY
○
○
○
○
○

09 WEDNESDAY

○
○
○
○
○
○
○
○

10 THURSDAY

○
○
○
○
○
○
○
○

11 FRIDAY

○
○
○
○
○
○
○
○

12 SATURDAY

○
○
○
○
○

13 SUNDAY

○
○
○
○
○
○
○
○

14 MONDAY

○
○
○
○
○
○
○
○

15 TUESDAY

○
○
○
○
○
○
○
○

16 WEDNESDAY

○
○
○
○
○

17 THURSDAY

○
○
○
○
○
○
○
○

18 FRIDAY

○
○
○
○
○
○
○
○

19 SATURDAY

○
○
○
○
○
○
○
○

20 SUNDAY

○
○
○
○
○

21 MONDAY

○
○
○
○
○
○
○
○

22 TUESDAY

○
○
○
○
○
○
○
○

23 WEDNESDAY

○
○
○
○
○
○
○
○

24 THURSDAY

○
○
○
○
○

25 FRIDAY

○
○
○
○
○
○
○
○

26 SATURDAY

○
○
○
○
○
○
○
○

27 SUNDAY

○
○
○
○
○
○
○
○

28 MONDAY

○
○
○
○
○

29 TUESDAY
○ _____
○ _____
○ _____
○ _____
○ _____
○ _____
○ _____
○ _____

30 WEDNESDAY
○ _____
○ _____
○ _____
○ _____
○ _____
○ _____
○ _____
○ _____

31 THURSDAY
○ _____
○ _____
○ _____
○ _____
○ _____
○ _____
○ _____
○ _____

NOTES

_____
_____
_____
_____
_____

November
2024

01 FRIDAY

- ○
- ○
- ○
- ○
- ○
- ○
- ○
- ○

02 SATURDAY

- ○
- ○
- ○
- ○
- ○
- ○
- ○
- ○

03 SUNDAY

- ○
- ○
- ○
- ○
- ○
- ○
- ○
- ○

04 MONDAY

- ○
- ○
- ○
- ○
- ○

05 TUESDAY

○
○
○
○
○
○
○
○

06 WEDNESDAY

○
○
○
○
○
○
○
○

07 THURSDAY

○
○
○
○
○
○
○
○

08 FRIDAY

○
○
○
○
○

November
2024

09 SATURDAY

○ _____
○ _____
○ _____
○ _____
○ _____
○ _____
○ _____
○ _____

10 SUNDAY

○ _____
○ _____
○ _____
○ _____
○ _____
○ _____
○ _____
○ _____

11 MONDAY

○ _____
○ _____
○ _____
○ _____
○ _____
○ _____
○ _____
○ _____

12 TUESDAY

○ _____
○ _____
○ _____
○ _____
○ _____

13 WEDNESDAY

○
○
○
○
○
○
○
○

14 THURSDAY

○
○
○
○
○
○
○
○
○

15 FRIDAY

○
○
○
○
○
○
○
○

16 SATURDAY

○
○
○
○
○

17 SUNDAY

○
○
○
○
○
○
○
○

18 MONDAY

○
○
○
○
○
○
○
○

19 TUESDAY

○
○
○
○
○
○
○
○

20 WEDNESDAY

○
○
○
○
○

21 THURSDAY

○
○
○
○
○
○
○
○

22 FRIDAY

○
○
○
○
○
○
○
○

23 SATURDAY

○
○
○
○
○
○
○
○

24 SUNDAY

○
○
○
○
○

25 MONDAY

○
○
○
○
○
○
○
○

26 TUESDAY

○
○
○
○
○
○
○
○

27 WEDNESDAY

○
○
○
○
○
○
○
○

28 THURSDAY

○
○
○
○
○

29 FRIDAY

○ _____
○ _____
○ _____
○ _____
○ _____
○ _____
○ _____
○ _____

30 SATURDAY

○ _____
○ _____
○ _____
○ _____
○ _____
○ _____
○ _____
○ _____

NOTES

_____
_____
_____
_____
_____
_____
_____
_____
_____
_____
_____
_____
_____
_____

December
2024

01 SUNDAY

○
○
○
○
○
○
○
○

02 MONDAY

○
○
○
○
○
○
○
○

03 TUESDAY

○
○
○
○
○
○
○
○

04 WEDNESDAY

○
○
○
○
○

05 THURSDAY

- ○ _____
- ○ _____
- ○ _____
- ○ _____
- ○ _____
- ○ _____
- ○ _____
- ○ _____

06 FRIDAY

- ○ _____
- ○ _____
- ○ _____
- ○ _____
- ○ _____
- ○ _____
- ○ _____
- ○ _____

07 SATURDAY

- ○ _____
- ○ _____
- ○ _____
- ○ _____
- ○ _____
- ○ _____
- ○ _____
- ○ _____

08 SUNDAY

- ○ _____
- ○ _____
- ○ _____
- ○ _____
- ○ _____

09 MONDAY

○ _____
○ _____
○ _____
○ _____
○ _____
○ _____
○ _____
○ _____

10 TUESDAY

○ _____
○ _____
○ _____
○ _____
○ _____
○ _____
○ _____
○ _____

11 WEDNESDAY

○ _____
○ _____
○ _____
○ _____
○ _____
○ _____
○ _____
○ _____

12 THURSDAY

○ _____
○ _____
○ _____
○ _____
○ _____

13 FRIDAY

○
○
○
○
○
○
○
○

14 SATURDAY

○
○
○
○
○
○
○
○

15 SUNDAY

○
○
○
○
○
○
○
○

16 MONDAY

○
○
○
○
○

17 TUESDAY

- ○
- ○
- ○
- ○
- ○
- ○
- ○
- ○

18 WEDNESDAY

- ○
- ○
- ○
- ○
- ○
- ○
- ○
- ○

19 THURSDAY

- ○
- ○
- ○
- ○
- ○
- ○
- ○
- ○

20 FRIDAY

- ○
- ○
- ○
- ○
- ○

21 SATURDAY

○ _____
○ _____
○ _____
○ _____
○ _____
○ _____
○ _____
○ _____

22 SUNDAY

○ _____
○ _____
○ _____
○ _____
○ _____
○ _____
○ _____
○ _____

23 MONDAY

○ _____
○ _____
○ _____
○ _____
○ _____
○ _____
○ _____
○ _____

24 TUESDAY

○ _____
○ _____
○ _____
○ _____
○ _____

25 WEDNESDAY

○
○ _____
○ _____
○ _____
○ _____
○ _____
○ _____
○ _____

26 THURSDAY

○
○ _____
○ _____
○ _____
○ _____
○ _____
○ _____
○ _____

27 FRIDAY

○
○ _____
○ _____
○ _____
○ _____
○ _____
○ _____
○ _____

28 SATURDAY

○
○ _____
○ _____
○ _____
○ _____

December
2024

29 SUNDAY
○ _____
○ _____
○ _____
○ _____
○ _____
○ _____
○ _____

30 MONDAY
○ _____
○ _____
○ _____
○ _____
○ _____
○ _____
○ _____
○ _____

31 TUESDAY
○ _____
○ _____
○ _____
○ _____
○ _____
○ _____
○ _____

NOTES

_____
_____
_____
_____
_____